POETRY EMOTIONS

Cumbria & Lancashire Poets

Edited By Emily Wilson

Years of

First published in Great Britain in 2016 by:

YoungWriters

Coltsfoot Drive
Peterborough
PE2 9BF
Telephone: 01733 890066
Website: www.youngwriters.co.uk

Foreword

Welcome Readers!

For our latest primary school competition we set school children nationwide a writing challenge - their challenge was to write a poem, and the theme was emotions. I am now proud to present Poetry Emotions – Cumbria & Lancashire Poets.

Within these pages you will find a variety of poetic styles from anger acrostics to sadness senses, from happy haikus to fear-provoking free verse. Some poems may leave you jumping for joy, some may tickle your sides while others may pull at your heart strings, testing your own emotions too!

The selection process, while difficult, proved to be a very rewarding task and I hope you enjoy the range of work that made it to the final stages. Our aim at Young Writers is to promote and encourage creativity in children and inspire a love for the written word. I hope seeing their work in print encourages our budding writers of the future further.

With so many wonderful poems featured in this anthology picking an overall winner was another very difficult task but I am happy to announce the winner from this collection is Tegan Lonsdale. I'd also like to congratulate all the young writers featured in this anthology. Finally, I hope you find the poems that lie within these pages just as entertaining as I did and I hope it is kept as a keepsake for many years to come.

Donna Samworth

Our charity partner for this academic year is ...

The voice for young people's **mental health and wellbeing**

We're aiming to raise a huge £5,000 this academic year to help raise awareness for YoungMinds and the great work they do to support children and young people.

If you would like to get involved visit
www.justgiving.com/Young-Writers

YoungMinds is the UK's leading charity committed to improving the emotional wellbeing and mental health of children and young people. They campaign, research and influence policy and practice on behalf of children and young people to improve care and services. They also provide expert knowledge to professionals, parents and young people through the Parents' Helpline, online resources, training and development, outreach work and publications. Their mission is to improve the emotional resilience of all children and to ensure that those who suffer ill mental health get fast and effective support.

www.youngminds.org.uk

Contents

Daniela Pilipavica (10)   52

Our Lady Of Lourdes Catholic Primary School, Manchester

Gabrielle Hughes (10)	53
Taylor Hudson (10)	54
Ciaran J Blake (11)	55
Ashton Wynne (10)	56
Marissa Wynne (10)	57
Alfie David Whatmough (11)	58
Rhonda Mcdonagh (10)	59
Betheny Leaf-Evans (11)	60
Harrison Joesph Tonge (9)	61
Jacob Hampson (9)	62
Taylor Graham (9)	63
Nathan Kabouadiko (10)	64
Holly Goodier (10)	65
Ben Hughes (11)	66
Oliver Hampson (9)	67
Kiera Lili Keegan (10)	68

St Leonard's CE Primary School, Preston

James Houghton (9)	69
Eva Jane Sealby (10)	70
Imogen Grace Shuttleworth (10)	71
Libby Wilton (8)	72
Patrick Johnose (10)	74
Jack Gillett (8)	75
Kelcey Kenworthy (9)	76
Alyssia Lane (10)	77
Ellis Cottam (10)	78
Isaac John Whitham (9) & Harry Chapman (9)	79
Marshall Edward Geirnaert	80
Angel Mirella Hill (8)	81
Katie Healy (11)	82

Will Aspinall (7)	83
Daniel Rimmer (10)	84
Ben Cookson (8)	85
Ruby-Lee Cottam (7)	86
Kylian Lobb	87
Isobel Barker	88
Rebecca Walsh (9)	89
Rio Steven Dewhurst (9)	90
Grace Bradley (9)	91
Aimee Dobson (9)	92
Amber Kennedy (11)	93
Matthew Barker (11)	94
Chloe Cowley (10)	95
Amy Trumper (9)	96
Matthew Clark (7)	97
Ailah Hamid (11)	98
Joel Bird (8)	99
Matthew Owen Mackie (10)	100
Amy Shamsuddin (10)	101
Hannah Shamsuddin (10)	102
Erin McEwan (9)	103
Holly Smith (11)	104
Ruby-May Graves (9)	105
Bradley Bowden	106
Freddie Masterson (7)	107
Lucy Ashton (8)	108
William Lane (8)	109
Daniel Smith (9)	110
Louis Wall (9)	111
Evelina Kazlauskaite-Lee (9)	112
Findley Dunne (8)	113
Lucy-Jane Bickerstaff (10)	114
Joshua McGee (11)	115
Megan Tinniswood (11)	116
Leo Lewis (10)	117
Lewis Hammonds (7)	118
Oliver Healy (10)	119
Joshua Cockburn (8)	120

Hannah Elizabeth Tuton (8)	121
Alice Wilton (8)	122
Amy Jessica Butler	123
Thomas Keith Myles (10)	124
Ellie Louise Barton (11)	125
Kai Jones	126
Imogen Crankshaw (9)	127
Phoebe Tinniswood (8)	128
Abigail Parker (8)	129
Zak Billington (7)	130
Amy Knight Garcia (9)	131
Harry Joe Noonan (9)	132
Hannah Sergeant (10)	133
Rebecca Freeman (11)	134
Josh Southern (10)	135
George Yerkess (10)	136
Jessica Hurst	137
George Holt (9)	138
Varissa Surti (9)	139
Oliver McGee	140
Jensen D C Hull (11)	141
William Thomas Steven (10)	142
Grace Connolly	143
Jack John Massey (11)	144
Jorja Simpson (9)	145
Benjamin Harmel (10)	146
Katie Hanna (9)	147
Joseph Benson (11)	148
Emilia Alice Fox (7)	149
Kathryn Lord (11)	150
Tom Ashton (7)	151
James Edward Steven (8)	152
Olivia Chatterton (9)	153
Reece Crossley (10)	154
Eleanor Jane Boardman (11)	155
Sam Craven (10)	156
James Robert Smith (10)	157
Ruby Guttridge (9)	158

Jacob Regan (8)	159
Charlie Smith (11)	160
Joshua Clifford (10)	161
Noah Patchell (10)	162

St Paul's CE Junior School, Barrow-In-Furness

Jensen Garnett (8)	163
Alessia Rigg (8)	164
Jay White (8)	165
Oliver Ducie (7)	166
Daniel Johnson (8)	167
Oliver Goodwin (7)	168
Cameron Duke (7)	169
Violet Bland (8)	170
Jamie Jackson (8)	171
Lily Rose Milburn (7)	172
Jordan Neale (7)	173
Reece Metcalfe (7)	174

The Poems

Well done! Your poem has been chosen as the best in this book.

The Buzz Of Excitement

Have you ever experienced the buzz that excitement
can bring?
Well, did you know, it's not just a human thing.

Picture the school on the first day of term,
The doors reaching out, as the students return.

Family car laden with holiday cases,
Radiator grill smiling, as it passes through places.

Nervous young couple on their first date,
Hinges squeak with pleasure, as they lean on the gate.

Presents piled high on Christmas morning,
Church bells ring, the children they're calling.

Last match of the season, as the teams line up,
Sun gleaming down on a very proud cup.

So next time you feel that buzz of excitement,
Remember this poem which brought
you enlightenment.

Tegan Jayne Lonsdale (11)
St Leonard's CE Primary School, Preston

Phew!

I am so excited that I'm walking in the posh
shopping mall
It looks exactly like a five-star hotel's hall
It took a few minutes to get to the treasure place
And then I found a black box next to the cup with a
diamond base

I felt extremely curious to see what was inside the box
The treasure must be behind at least one
hundred locks
Just as I was about to grab it and buy it
Another man grabbed it and his face went and lit

I wasn't just angry, I was furious
No one can recognise a moment ago I was curious
I shouted and screamed and I kicked the chair
And I even took some scissors and shaved off a
man's hair!

After a long time I finally calmed down
And I was proud because my anger and my frown went
out of town
A baby pointed at me and said, 'Da, do, da!'
As I put my hands in the air and I shouted, 'Hallelujah!'

Everyone stared at me like an owl
I can feel the embarrassment monster in me going
on a prowl
As I covered myself I immediately fled
And then I went, 'Phew,' that's what I said.

Adrian Wong (10)
Clevelands Preparatory School, Bolton

Moody

Happy and Merry come along doing joyful activities
But soon they hear a noise, it is big and *bang!*
It's Clumsy and Embarrassed
Their hands are like butter and their cheeks
are tomatoes
They are klutzy
But when they go home they are the loneliest
people around

Uuuh! It's Grumpy and Sad
Grumpy and Sad are wet, soggy and never want
to play
They are always on the way to let down the day
By sulking and pouting
Oh no, it's Disgust and Angry, they are the worst

Disgust is the disgusting one,
She hates all her greens
She will never let me eat them
That's how mean she is
Angry is so bad, he never lets out the blues
He is big, fierce and spiky and only Happy and Merry
let out the blues

Merry and Happy are my best because they brighten up my day.

Sophia Raana Hasan Aftab (10)
Clevelands Preparatory School, Bolton

Happy

My face is so happy,
I cannot wait for school.
Writing is the best thing,
But I love being on my own.
I love reading and art
I like the park and baking.
Chocolate cake is the best!
When I get home I have to see
The crazy cat Fearne.
Then I go to the beach,
Then a stroll back home,
I am happy when I go in my bedroom.

Faye Emma Tennent (10)
Clevelands Preparatory School, Bolton

Curiosity

Yesterday I wondered
Why is the sky so blue?
And how did the gum get on my shoe?
How do people climb trees?
And will my brother be taller than me?

Today I pondered
Who invented time?
And how do poets rhyme?
How do rockets get to those heights?
And why do people go on flights?

Tomorrow I might discover
How far do Frisbees go?
And why do snails go so slow?
Will I find the answers in the morning?
Why am I so curious about everything?

Harvey Dhokia (10)
Clevelands Preparatory School, Bolton

Ski Countdown

Three days to go, I can't believe I'm going skiing
But this is only the beginning

Two days to go, I'm that excited I feel sick
Anyway, it better go quick

One day to go I feel a tingle in my body
I feel the excitement monster's getting to me

No days to go, finally the day I go skiing and I'm here, I
could scream!
I have so many hopes, thinking about going down
the slopes
With snowflakes landing on my nose
Ending up facing at my toes.

Eloise Jae Gibbs (10)
Clevelands Preparatory School, Bolton

Anger Man

Anger is a devil sometimes invisible
Being a naughty person to whoever he sees
Comes out to people as nice as they could be
Takes them down nearly breaking their knees
Like a rugby player

Boys and girls run away
Never dare to be mean
They need to calm him down
Take deep breaths
Hope he doesn't come back

People don't see him a lot
He lives deep down underground
Sneaks up on people, making them shout out loud.

Robin Jaaskelainen (10)
Clevelands Preparatory School, Bolton

Happy

Sour sweets are tangy and tickle my tongue
They are lots of fun to eat.
The beautiful hot golden sun
Shining brightly in the blue sky.
I feel playful and ready for adventure.
Birds singing, 'Good morning' to each other
Flying and swooping from nest to nest
To feed the tiny chicks.
My heart is beating like a drum with excitement.
I love soft and silky Sparky in his comfy little bed,
He makes me smile and I feel eager to play with him.

Susanne Perry (9)
Clevelands Preparatory School, Bolton

Happiness

Happiness is one of the greatest emotions of them all
And makes you feel jumpy inside
Happiness makes my eyes light up like stars
And feels like I'm floating on Mars
Happiness is sunny days and clear blue skies
Clouds like fluffy cotton wool hovering gracefully by
Like how my mum makes me feel when I'm around her
Happiness is a feeling tingling through my bones
Happiness helps us talk in cheerful tones.

Zain Mehraj (10)
Clevelands Preparatory School, Bolton

The Sky At Night

The sky is as black as a bin bag
My eyes are starting to close
My body is closing down
The lovely day is gone
The TV's on, I should turn it off
I know I can't be bothered
But electric bills are a lot of money
It could be worth millions
My happy face will turn into a frown
If I don't, send me to bed
Turn it off and put my sleepy head to bed.

Isabel Freya Heyes (9)
Clevelands Preparatory School, Bolton

You're Enough As You Are...

Don't feel down
Just because of others
Don't have a frown
Just because you feel the need to hide from reality

Even though others say
They understand you
They might think about you in a different way
Think about it, it's true

Others might drag you out
Of your real personality
But don't have any self-doubt
It will be okay

No one should be picked on
Because of who they are
Don't bully at all
Don't let it go too far...

You're enough as you are!

Chloë Hodgson (10)
Newlaithes Junior School, Carlisle

What Is This Feeling?

It's the middle of the night
Out my window a light flashed bright
A noise, a rumble
Maybe it's just my tummy having a grumble
I'm shaking down to the bone
I think I'm turning... to stone
I creep to the window, peep through the curtain
I need to see, I need to be certain
If what I think is true
But at the first sight
Of the bright light
I get an incredible fright
Back under my covers my mind is reeling
What is this feeling?

Katrina Struthers (10)
Newlaithes Junior School, Carlisle

Feeling Down

F eeling down is the worst feeling ever

E veryone has a down day

E ven animals feel down sometimes

L ook on the bright side

I n the end it will get better

N obody should feel down

G o to someone to make you feel happy again!

D on't make anyone else feel down as well

O nly feel down if you have to

W herever, whenever you might feel down

N ever put yourself down just because of it!

Charlie Morris (10)
Newlaithes Junior School, Carlisle

The Goal

Being on a team of
Ten others
Can make me feel
Like they're my brothers

The ball gets passed
Back and fro
Then the ball is mine
And I get a go

The goal in sight
I can see the light
I smash the ball
And I score a goal!

I feel delight
My heart is bright
I know my team
Will give a mighty fight.

Mikey Kehoe (9)
Newlaithes Junior School, Carlisle

Happy Holidays

H appiness is splashing in the cool blue pool

O utside having picnics on the beach

L oving the Spanish heat

I ce creams lovely and cold

D ancing in the club, to your favourite songs

A lways put suncream on, you don't want sunburn

Y ellow like a banana is the colour of the sun

S wimming in the sea, in the middle of the day.

Ellen Jane Sheals (10)
Newlaithes Junior School, Carlisle

Dance

I love to dance
It makes me so happy
Whenever I hear music
My feet start tapping

I love to dance
My dance teacher inspires me
Doesn't matter if you're on the back line
Just try your hardest

I love to dance
Ballet, tap and cheer
Hip hop, street and freestyle
It's all at Carlisle Dance Academy.

Freya Sindall (10)
Newlaithes Junior School, Carlisle

Happiness

H appiness is just the greatest

A lways try to have a fun time

P laying on my trampoline, free as a blackbird

P ogo sticks are super bouncy

I ndoor fun on rainy days

N ice weather means sunny holidays

E veryone deserves to be happy

S weets and chocolate are the greatest treats

S o let's all be happy every day!

Niamh Hewitson (10)
Newlaithes Junior School, Carlisle

Holiday

Excited to be going on...

H appy as can be, swimming in the sea

O lives on a pizza to be eaten for my tea

L azy days in the sun, trying not to burn my bum!

I n the pool I like to swim

D ad plays ball with me and my sister

A mazing times when we're away

Y es, holidays are the best time ever!

Rhys Wilding (10)
Newlaithes Junior School, Carlisle

Happiness

Happiness is the sun that shines bright
Happiness is the wind that blows my kite
Happiness is eating ice cream and cake
Happiness is being in the kitchen learning how to bake
Happiness is going to my grandma's house
Happiness is seeing a little fieldmouse
Happiness is going to the park to play
Happiness makes me happy all day.

Samantha Mattinson (10)
Newlaithes Junior School, Carlisle

Feeling Blue

When I'm feeling blue
I'm stuck to the spot like glue
I can't feel tall
I feel so small
I'm just not happy at all
When I'm feeling droopy
I also feel so gloopy
I want to crawl in a hole
And dig further like a mole
I feel alone, I feel no joy
I think I might have to play with a boy.

Millie-Mae Thompson (10)
Newlaithes Junior School, Carlisle

Emotions

E very time I am sad, I cry

M ost times I'm happy and laugh

O n Saturdays I'm excited for football

T he best emotion is feeling loved

I hate to feel pain

O n my birthday I like to be surprised

N othing can stop me from having emotions.

Jack Dudley (10)
Newlaithes Junior School, Carlisle

How Am I Feeling?

My frown lines are as deep as the ocean
My face is blood-red
The volcano in my stomach is about to erupt
Hot air blows out of my nostrils, like a dragon
breathing fire
My fists are clenched as if ready to punch
My mouth screams!
What is this feeling?

Niamh Harkness (10)
Newlaithes Junior School, Carlisle

Happiness And Joy

Happiness is the greatest thing ever
It fills you with joy
It makes you feel good inside
Joy, greatness, excitement and pride
You will know you're fine when you have happiness
and joy
And always remember that you have happiness
And you really need joy.

Holly Pieroway (10)
Newlaithes Junior School, Carlisle

When I'm Feeling Scared!

When you're feeling scared
You should always be prepared
At lunchtime don't be scared of ham
But maybe Spam

Always tell your parents this
Or they might give you a fist
When you lay down your head
Get nice and cuddly in your bed.

Evie Bell (9)
Newlaithes Junior School, Carlisle

The Anger Arisen

On a summer's day I thought I would play with a boy
But I never because it is hard
No one likes me
When I get angry it feels like I am digging a hole
of darkness
And I feel angry enough to shoot fireworks
I think I need to play with a girl for once!

Clinton Liam Kelton (10)
Newlaithes Junior School, Carlisle

Summer

S ummer is the time of nature and plants

U nlikely to be dark, gloomy and grey

M other Nature comes out to play

M emories and moments are made

E very summer gets better and better

R emember to always have fun in the summer!

Jemma Salkeld (10)
Newlaithes Junior School, Carlisle

I Like Football

I like football
I like it a lot
I play for a team
My football boots are green
I score lots of goals
In the right holes
I like to kick the ball
And sometimes I fall
Football is my life
It might even come before my wife.

Jack Glendinning (9)
Newlaithes Junior School, Carlisle

Scared

S ometimes people are scared

C ouldn't we help them

A re you one of them?

R eaction is important

E ven animals get scared

D on't react badly.

Chelsey Morris (10)
Newlaithes Junior School, Carlisle

Calm As The Ocean

As calm as the sea
Or as calm as the wind
Happy as the sun
Shining very brightly
As wet as the rain
Or as deep as the ocean
The only way to feel
Is as happy as me.

Joshua Pritchard (9)
Newlaithes Junior School, Carlisle

The Great War - Haiku

Yelling farewell now
Wondering if I will live
Will life continue?

I am on the train
Ready to see what happens
I'm giving my life

Will my friends survive?
Will I be alone or not?
Goodbye everyone

Preparing for war
Holding my gun and ready
Saving my country

This is not the end
Fighting for my country is
The least I will do

War is exciting
But can be terrifying
But it's still worthwhile.

Ben Morley (9)
North Lakes School, Penrith

The Great War! - Haiku

Goodbye, farewell now
Anxious about the future
Will they all come back?

Tearful and upset
People's tears are like raindrops
Where will they be sent?

Lots of people shocked
Lots of people heartbroken
Depressed and lonely

Down-hearted people
People are upset badly
What will happen next?

Molly Guy-Gregg (10)
North Lakes School, Penrith

The Great War - Haiku

Goodbye, farewell now
I hope we win the great war
What might happen now?

Terrified for war
My heart is a locked-up safe
Opened by your love

Tears are waterfalls
Do you have to leave us now?
Suffering at war

We're ready to fight
Dad, we don't want to lose you
We need to rush now.

Jessica Gemmell (10)
North Lakes School, Penrith

The Great War - Haiku

Lovingly hugging
My heart splitting into two
Sadly letting go

Weeping sadly now
Watching him leave me alone
Hoping he returns

Please don't leave us, Dad
Tears fall like a waterfall
Please don't let us down

Excited for war
Training, travelling with friends
Where will we be sent?

Grace Godolphin (9)
North Lakes School, Penrith

The Great War

Farewell family
Hugging, rushing and crying
What might happen next?

Excited to win
Hearts broke from loss and sadness
What will it be like?

Upset families
Children are feeling so sad
It was for the best

Suffering at war
Ready to fight in the war
Hopefully to win!

Mia Wyllie (10)
North Lakes School, Penrith

Haiku

Leaping, having fun
He is a loud, leaping lamb
He wraps you in warmth

Tiptoeing to me
Fear floats boldly behind me
Fear creeps secretly

You're miserable
Sadness brings tears every day
You are all alone

Anger exploded
Erupting destructively
A deep, dark, loud hole.

Amy Thompson (9)
North Lakes School, Penrith

The Great War! - Haiku

Goodbye, farewell now
Scared, anxious for the future
Lovingly hugging

Depressed about war
Thinking if they will go home
Terrified people

People wait for their husbands
Petrified people are sad
Heartbroken people

Down-hearted people
People are upset badly
What will happen now?

Alyssa Rose Simpson (10)
North Lakes School, Penrith

The Great War - Haiku

Goodbye, farewell now
Gone to the great war ahead
Scared that I might die

Risky in the war
Suffering with my disease
I hope the war ends

Germans are rebels
Bombers are bombing but the
British take over

The guns are loaded
We are ready in the war...
Many people die.

Max Currie (10)
North Lakes School, Penrith

The Great War - Haiku

Goodbye, farewell now
Anxious about the future
Lovingly hugging

Depressed about war
Thinking about those in war
Weeping about him

Upset he might die
Like a person full of tears
Crying so sadly

Terrified of death
Will they see each other now?
What will happen now?

Darcie Bidgood (10)
North Lakes School, Penrith

World War I - Haiku

Goodbye, farewell now
Getting the guns ready now
Packing up our stuff

Travelling with friends
Everyone went to the war
I fought for Britain

We dug big trenches
All us soldiers hid in them
Some had a trench full.

Sonny Kelly (9)
North Lakes School, Penrith

The Great War - Haiku

Goodbye, farewell now
My safe opened with your love
What will you do next?

Ready for the war
Prepared as well as worried
Where am I going?

Saying farewell now
Please do not leave us now Dad
We will miss you Dad.

Keelie Louise Thompson (10)
North Lakes School, Penrith

Anger And Fear - Haiku

Anger's violent
Storming like a raging bull
No more happiness

Fear makes me leap high
Squealing in a high-pitched voice
Bravely crawling close.

Jasmine Bellas (10)
North Lakes School, Penrith

Anger - Haiku

Hot, intense red mist
Pacing like a savage beast
It's a vicious flash!

Anger storms with rage
It rushed around, boiling blood
Anger's violent...

Anya Martin (9)
North Lakes School, Penrith

Anger And Fear! - Haiku

Anger is red-hot
Raging like an eruption
Thumps furiously...

Fear is so painful
Squealing like an angry pig
Coy, troubled with grief...

Holly Oakey (9)
North Lakes School, Penrith

Anger - Haiku

Anger's furious
Sneakily leaps through bodies
As fast as a train

Annoyingly gripped
Like a magnet to my head
Deep down I'm angry.

Sonny Askins (10)
North Lakes School, Penrith

Anger And Fear - Haiku

Anger struck wildly
Like an outraged volcano
Troubled at midnight...

Fear crept silently
It shook my delicate spine
And forever stayed...

Lexi Hodgson (9)
North Lakes School, Penrith

Anger And Fear - Haiku

Anger deep and cold
Annoyingly irritates
Makes you sweat with rage!

Fear has struck at me
Deep in my body it lies
Curled up in a ball.

Jackson Woof (9)
North Lakes School, Penrith

Anger And Fear - Haiku

Volcanoes erupt
Like a raging, harmful beast
Anger is intense...

Fear is the worst thing
Fear is a big, big barrel
We see fun again.

Alfie Brennand (9)
North Lakes School, Penrith

The Great War - Haiku

Anger storms with rage
He boils like a volcano
He silently stomps...

Sneaking timidly
Fear hovers up behind me...
Jealous of safety!

Rianna Harrison (10)
North Lakes School, Penrith

The Great War - Haiku

Anger boils your blood
Like a fearsome raging bull
Grieving in despair

Scared like a black cat
Fear crept into me darkly
Uncontrollably.

Melissa Clark (9)
North Lakes School, Penrith

Anger - Haiku

Furious lightning!
Dark, storming, gripping black clouds
Red-hot and breathless.

Daniela Pilipavica (10)
North Lakes School, Penrith

Untitled

I just don't know what to do!
I am feeling emotional today,
Part of me wants to shout hooray!
But part of me wants to hide away,
I just don't know what to do.
I can feel a prickling in my thoughts,
I want to cry and I don't.
I just want to sail away on a boat,
I just don't know what to do.
I want to cry and sob all day,
I want to go and run away.
But I want to laugh and dance and have a say,
I just don't know what to do.
These are my emotions I wanted to share,
Sometimes I really want to rip out my hair,
Because the people around me just don't care,
I just don't know what to do.

Gabrielle Hughes (10)
Our Lady Of Lourdes Catholic Primary School, Manchester

Happy

H is for happiness when I win a trophy,
   I jump up in the air like I just don't care.
A is animated when I feel excited,
   I like to express myself, showing lots of joy.
P is for pleased when I received my handwriting pen,
   I felt very proud that I wanted to scream out loud.
P is for pleasant when I smile as wide as a lake,
   I make everyone happy because they see my
   pleasant smile.
Y is for yell to cheer someone on during a race,
   To help them get to base.

Taylor Hudson (10)
Our Lady Of Lourdes Catholic Primary School, Manchester

Happiness

If happiness were a colour,
It would be white,
As white as clouds that
Roam the free skies.

If happiness were a taste,
It would be delicious,
As delicious as ice cream on a
Hot summer's day.

If happiness were a smell,
It would be scrumptious,
As scrumptious as freshly-
Made doughnuts.

If happiness were a sound,
It would be quiet,
As quiet as a lonely bird flying
In an empty forest.

If happiness were human,
They would be hyper,
As hyper as a toddler being
A total nutter.

Ciaran J Blake (11)
Our Lady Of Lourdes Catholic Primary School, Manchester

Emotions Of Life

Sadness,
Sadness makes me think of darkness.
It is like you're a storm,
Getting ready to get un-warm

Mad,
Mad reminds me of my dad.
It is like two wrestlers getting out of hand,
And one of them had a bad land.

Happy,
Happy makes me think of the birds that are flappy.
It is like when you have a fun day,
On your own holiday.

Joy,
Joy reminds me of my first toy.
It is like getting your phone back,
From losing it in your backpack.

Ashton Wynne (10)
Our Lady Of Lourdes Catholic Primary School, Manchester

Feelings Of Life

What do you feel?
I feel sad, upset and dull
What about you my son?
I feel nauseous when I am full!
Are you happy, excited or ecstatic?
I love my family and friends,
Whenever I feel clappy.
I feel happy when trees are sappy,
But I think trees are saddy.
I am disappointed with everyone now,
Because I am a teacher it's pretty swell,
I tell children off for not doing their work,
And I joke with the teachers while I smirk.
Follow your dreams and treasure moments forever.

Marissa Wynne (10)
Our Lady Of Lourdes Catholic Primary School, Manchester

Family

F amily is so important to me, they make me feel gleeful.

A lthough I have annoying siblings who make me feel vexed.

M y mum and dad are the best, I feel spoilt with them around.

I will love them with all of my heart.

L onely I will never feel when I am with my family.

Y ou would be so lucky if your family was like mine.

This family is mine.
For a very long time.
Always with me.
They always make me merry.

I love my family.

Alfie David Whatmough (11)
Our Lady Of Lourdes Catholic Primary School, Manchester

Sad

One day I was glad,
But then my emotions turned to sad.
My heart felt crushed,
And my face went blushed.

I fell off the boat,
And got a lump in my throat.
Everyone laughed but I felt lonely,
Sad, devastated and in tears.

My mum said never mind,
But I felt like I was left behind.
In my mind no one was being kind.
Everyone calls me blind because I wear glasses,
But I thought to myself, *never mind*.

Rhonda Mcdonagh (10)
Our Lady Of Lourdes Catholic Primary School, Manchester

Calmness

C alming music that soothes my ears

A ll along the way I want it to be

L aying in bed as floppy as a sloth

M y heart is full of bright colours inside

N ever felt so relaxed now I have had a long bath

E very single day I hear birds singing

S waying on a large, snug hammock

S mooth, comfy blanket cuddling me.

Betheny Leaf-Evans (11)
Our Lady Of Lourdes Catholic Primary School, Manchester

Furious

F ury comes out of me like a bullet

U mbrellas to protect you from me

R eact quickly I'm going to burst

I 'll regret what I've done,

O ur lives will fade and you'll lose control

U mbrellas won't last

S oon it will end but my temper will last.

Harrison Joesph Tonge (9)
Our Lady Of Lourdes Catholic Primary School, Manchester

Anger

A is for anger, it makes me feel like there are flames in my head,

N is for naughty behaviour when you're mad,

G is for growling when someone says something mean to you,

E is for emotions, they are your feelings,

R is for rage, it means you get really, really angry.

Jacob Hampson (9)

Our Lady Of Lourdes Catholic Primary School, Manchester

Furious

F ull of anger,

U rging to scream,

R acing to go home to my bed to be alone,

I 've finally got home, I'm in my room,

O bviously nobody is coming in my room,

U nless I call for help,

S o it's a new day and I am happy with my friends.

Taylor Graham (9)
Our Lady Of Lourdes Catholic Primary School, Manchester

Angry

A ntisocial behaviour makes me snap,

N ot being able to play football makes my temper rise up

G oing shopping annoys me,

R ed bulls take advantage of me when I snap,

Y ou do not want your temper to get advantage of you or else you'll get in trouble.

Nathan Kabouadiko (10)
Our Lady Of Lourdes Catholic Primary School, Manchester

Untitled

When people bully and they say you didn't floss,
The bubbling in my throat is me feeling cross.
The rage inside me is ready to burst ,
On these days I would rather be cursed.
However, I figure I should let it go,
Now my anger level has dropped down low.

Holly Goodier (10)
Our Lady Of Lourdes Catholic Primary School, Manchester

Untitled

My dog Frankie died
I am sad:
My dog Frankie died,
And I cried,
I cried all night,
Like my dog bites,
I went all itchy,
So I called my friend Mitchy,
I told him the news,
Which gave him the blues.

Ben Hughes (11)
Our Lady Of Lourdes Catholic Primary School, Manchester

Happy

H is for high spirits, a new game,

A is for a giggle as it's funny,

P is for pleased for my high score,

P is for perfect,

Y is for yes, I am on my iPad.

Oliver Hampson (9)
Our Lady Of Lourdes Catholic Primary School, Manchester

Nature - Haiku

Seeing trees swaying
In the wind, dancing for joy,
As the grass joins in.

Kiera Lili Keegan (10)
Our Lady Of Lourdes Catholic Primary School, Manchester

Emotions Poem

Sadness is the waves of tears and sobbing,
Happiness is the magic that flows through us all.
A sprinkle of joy is what everybody needs,
To stop us from bursting into a bawl.

Being nervous or anxious is what some people do,
Or sometimes they're excited or willing to be on
the stage.
Sometimes they feel like hiding behind the props,
But others just want to be the main sage.

Sisters are usually the grump of the pack,
And the brothers always shine out with light.
So remember, if you're grumpy or cheerful,
You are either the dark or the bright.

James Houghton (9)
St Leonard's CE Primary School, Preston

Anger

Anger looks like dull grey clouds
And large red spikes
And is a huge warning.
Anger feels like a ginormous volcano
Erupting loudly and fiercely.
When people are angry, they shout sharply
And anger breaks people's hearts
And feelings.
Anger tastes like bitter grapefruit,
Running through your throat.
Anger sounds sometimes
Like smashing and breaking things up.
Anger is something
Not nice to have.

Eva Jane Sealby (10)
St Leonard's CE Primary School, Preston

Anger

I am confident, not shy,
I don't laugh or cry,
I can't help feeling this way,
I am like this every day.

People tell me to stop and to count to three,
But I can't help this fire that's inside of me,
I don't listen to what anyone says,
My whole mind is a puzzling maze.

Some kind of rage just comes through me,
Please, oh please just let me be free,
I don't think about what I do or say,
But what I do is their price to pay.

I am the feeling which has no heart,
I just want to tear everything apart,
I don't get scared, happy or sad,
Because I am Anger and I am always mad.

Imogen Grace Shuttleworth (10)
St Leonard's CE Primary School, Preston

Eating Emotions

Bright and beautiful
Just like a flower,
Happiness has talents
And its own special power.

Sadness is like
Drifting along the sea,
There are many downs
But everyone can be happy.

I'm happy when I dance,
The straight and the curves,
I feel so free,
And can let go of my nerves.

Think of the people
That make you happy,
Follow their path
And make sure you're happy.

You can be happy
In the saddest of times,
And sad
In the happy times.

Eating your emotions
Is the best thing to do,
But make sure
You always try something new!

Libby Wilton (8)
St Leonard's CE Primary School, Preston

Jolly Joy

Joy, happiness, excitement too,
Makes everyone smile, such as me and you.
You feel joy when summer's round the corner,
You also feel joy when you are in a hot sauna.
Joy is when you are getting a dog,
Also watching badgers playing in a log.
You can tell someone's happy when they have a
great smile,
Like when they laugh and giggle for a while.
There's also happiness in getting a new friend,
And when they tell you friendship will never end.
Like Jesus, joy is the light of the world,
But to girls it is getting their hair curled.
To most boys it's getting a new football kit,
And having Neymar or Messi written on the back of it.

Patrick Johnose (10)
St Leonard's CE Primary School, Preston

My First Plane Journey

My mum and dad booked a holiday abroad
And I was full of worry.

I'd never been on a plane before
And I didn't want the holiday to hurry.

When I walked onto the plane,
I felt nervous but also excited.

It was as long as a football pitch
It was like being at Manchester United.

When the plane set off
I was as white as a ghost.

But as it went up in the air
I was happy, more than most.

I landed in Portugal
The plane's wheels touched the ground.

I was proud of how I overcame
The aeroplane's sound.

Jack Gillett (8)
St Leonard's CE Primary School, Preston

What Emotion Am I?

I can do it,
Yes I can,
They can't,
I'm sure I can.

I can do it,
I'm on fire,
My levels keep getting higher and higher!

I won't sleep,
They will weep,
I'll go right to the top,
I won't stop,
They don't stand a chance,
So then I'll do my celebration dance.

It will be easy, exhausting, but it might come true.
Just think when I'll be there,
Stood high up in the air.
I'll be standing on number one,
Holding a trophy,
Wearing a medal,
Then my job will be done!

What emotion am I?

Kelcey Kenworthy (9)
St Leonard's CE Primary School, Preston

St Leonard's Spectacular School Poem

St Leonard's School is super fun,
Monday has only just begun,
Three playtimes a day for singing and dancing
Now you can shout hooray!
Because today was a good day.

St Leonard's School is super fun,
Tuesday has only just begun,
Dinner time's the best today
You might even shout yeah.

St Leonard's School is super fun,
Wednesday has only just begun,
Grass and swings and other things,
Thursday night tomorrow so collect up your things.

St Leonard's School is super fun,
Friday has only just done,
Weekend to laugh and dine,
And BBQ in the sunshine.

Alyssia Lane (10)
St Leonard's CE Primary School, Preston

The Wonderful World Of Walt Disney, Florida!

I've been to a place called Florida,
It's a long way away in the sun,
There's a place called The Magic Kingdom,
Full of wonders, surprises and fun!

I've met all the Disney characters,
Including Magic Mickey Mouse,
We stayed in a villa with a pool,
What fun we had in that house!

I've experienced The Animal Kingdom,
Sea World, Epcot and all the rest!
All were very exciting,
Still can't decide which was best.

I'm now home with happy memories
Of a place where the skies were blue,
Thank you Walt Disney and friends,
Dreams really do come true!

Ellis Cottam (10)
St Leonard's CE Primary School, Preston

Summertime

S ummertime is fun time

U nder the crashing waves in the beautiful blue sea are colourful tropical fish going through the colourful reef

M editerranean sea tickles my toes as I swiftly walk down the beach

M um sunbathes in the back garden in her bright, colourful bikini while I play football

E very night I am in the garden eating yummy BBQs

R unning around with friends is what I do, having water fights

T ents put up by the dads while mums sit chatting in the sun

I ce cream all over my face is what I eat

M um loves to garden when it is sunny whilst I play football

E very time the sun shines it makes me happy.

Isaac John Whitham (9) & Harry Chapman (9)
St Leonard's CE Primary School, Preston

Happy Harry

Harry happy,
Harry sad,
Harry good,
Harry bad,
Skipping along,
Singing a song,
His name is Happy Harry!

Harry happy,
Harry sad,
Harry good,
Harry bad,
He is filled with laughter,
But naughty always after.
His name is Happy Harry.

Marshall Edward Geirnaert
St Leonard's CE Primary School, Preston

Happiness

H appiness is something that you bring to life.

A musement is always laughing and having a smile on your face.

P layfulness is an openness to anything that may happen.

P aradise is where you are right now.

I n a good mood is never letting things drag you down.

N ever been better, feeling so great.

E xhilaration is that feeling you get just after a great idea hits you and just before you realise what's wrong with it.

S ister is more than a forever friend. She is joy to the heart and love without end. She brings such happiness.

S atisfaction, one's curiosity is one of the greatest sources of happiness in life.

Angel Mirella Hill (8)
St Leonard's CE Primary School, Preston

Anger!

If anger were a colour, it would be red,
As red as a ball of fire in the middle of the darkness.

If anger were a taste, it would be a red-hot chilli,
Making your mouth feel like it is on fire.

If anger were a smell, it would be burning plastic,
Whose grey, gloomy fumes fill the sky.

If anger were a sound, it would be an irritable and
repetitive noise,
Turned up too loud.

If I had to choose what anger looked like,
It would be a black, cloudy sky just before a
thunderstorm.

If anger were a feeling, it would be gritting your teeth
And clenching your fists.

Katie Healy (11)
St Leonard's CE Primary School, Preston

Cool Bob

There oncE was a guy called Bob

He tried his utMost to be cool

He hated school mOre than others

You see our Bob was Terribly shy around girls

The thought of kIssing them excited him

But he felt nervOus talking to them

One day the Nicest girl in school kissed him

Bob became the cooleSt boy in school and he was overjoyed.

Will Aspinall (7)
St Leonard's CE Primary School, Preston

Happy

Happy tastes good,
Happy feels exciting,
It is a big face with a smile on it,
Happy is birthday surprises,
Happy is scoring goals,
Happy is winning the league,
Happy is playing with the dog,
Happy is my dog's tail wagging,
Happy is going on new adventures,
Happy is jumping in the pool,
Happy is fresh air,
Happy is fantastic.

Daniel Rimmer (10)
St Leonard's CE Primary School, Preston

The Lion's Lair

As I was walking through the jungle,
I suddenly heard a cracking sound.
I looked down and saw that I had accidentally stood on
a slimy slug.

Over in the distance, I could see enormous elephants
rolling in the mud,
The mud looked like chocolate.
Next, I saw a slithery snake,
I hid behind the largest tree I could find, because I
was scared.
Shortly afterwards, I saw an orange orangutan,
It was colossal.
The tree which the orangutan was in was as tall
as a mountain.
Suddenly, I heard a loud *rooaarrr!*
Then I realised I was in the lion's lair.
I felt very frightened!

Ben Cookson (8)
St Leonard's CE Primary School, Preston

Grandma And Grandad's Magical Surprise

Grandma and Grandad called in to visit to tell us a change of plan,
'Surprise! We are going to Disney World Florida and not the caravan!'
I felt happy and excited, wondering what I would do and see.
An adventure was waiting for my family and me.
We visited the Disney parks, Seaworld and more,
I was filled with happiness with so much to explore.
I've met Mickey and Minnie Mouse and watched big fireworks go boom,
I've watched Anna and Elsa sing and snowflakes filled the room,
I've petted the beautiful dolphins which were lovely and smooth to touch.
Thank you, Grandma and Grandad, I love you very much.

Ruby-Lee Cottam (7)
St Leonard's CE Primary School, Preston

Anger

Anger, please go away,
On this sunny day in May,
I don't want you to be here,
Am I making myself clear?

Anger, please go away,
You're getting on my nerves today,
I just want to be happy and free,
With a smile on my face, full of glee.

Anger, please go away,
I just want to play today,
Anger, you always make me feel sad,
And that can make me behave bad.

Anger, please go away,
I know you can't stay,
I don't know where you actually belong,
But I do know when you are here, you make
me feel wrong.

Kylian Lobb
St Leonard's CE Primary School, Preston

Happiness

The sound of birds singing
Going to the park and swinging
Meeting friends not seen for a long time
Keeping hands away from slime
The taste of sweets and chocolate
Dodging rain, every droplet
The splash at the end of a water slide
Sledging down a hillside
Giving and receiving hugs
Avoiding sticky, slimy slugs
Playing in the fresh snow
Going to a Disney show
Picking flowers from the garden
Not having to say pardon
The smell of a rose and of flowers
Staying in the shower for hours
The warm sun on your skin
Giving gifts to your kin.

Isobel Barker
St Leonard's CE Primary School, Preston

Happy

Roses are red
Violets are blue
I'm so happy
When I'm with you

I'm happy when I'm with you
Because you never make me feel blue

I'm happy when it's sunny
I'm happy when it snows
I'm happy with all four seasons
Even when it blows.

Rebecca Walsh (9)
St Leonard's CE Primary School, Preston

What Emotion Am I?

It lives in a freaky, dark, deep forest
And it gets ready to kill, to eat and to bite
They sit in the corner moaning
And it tries to punch and have a fight.
It lights up when it's ready to punch
And its head blasts up like a volcano.
People run away screaming and dreaming
Which must be awful.
His eyes light up like a light
When he says, 'Oh my!'
Then he catches his prey, prey, prey.
People go to it every day, day, day,
They kill the wonderful, ugly creature.
That's why they don't like anybody today.
What emotion am I?

Rio Steven Dewhurst (9)
St Leonard's CE Primary School, Preston

Embarrassment

My family went out for tea
I took my friend Lucy with me,
My family then started to dance
And I started to get embarrassed.
They called it the bottom shuffle
My cousin then started to film it.
I went as red as a giant tomato.

I was so humiliated
I was blushing, I went so red.
My friends were laughing at my mum
Lucy witnessed my mum's bad dancing.
My cousin put it on YouTube
I felt like the world was looking at me.
I was extremely ashamed
Self-conscious and I was blushing
Until we became famous on YouTube.

Grace Bradley (9)
St Leonard's CE Primary School, Preston

Jumpy Joy

Joyful, jumpy joy is like a bouncy toy,
Joy comes to help people when they're feeling down,
She is like a spring and her hair is brown,
She lives high above the clouds,
I am cheerful when she comes,
And she is loved by the crowd.

'Oh Joy, you don't know how miserable we feel when
you go.'
Joy says, 'I have to go, but I will come back soon
I hope.'
Joy always has a smile on her face,
Although she has a pile of frowns to turn upside down,
She thinks it's ace every time she goes to a
different place.

Aimee Dobson (9)
St Leonard's CE Primary School, Preston

Love Is...

Love is when someone is stuck in your mind,
It is when there is a name you can't leave behind.
Love is when you have a strong passion for others,
You can also feel it towards your sisters and brothers.
Pink or red is the colour of love,
Another symbol could be a dove.
Not a single body does love not appear in,
I'm afraid you can't put it in the bin.
If love were a picture it would be a heart,
A heart that could never ever be torn apart.
Love is the glistening sparkle in your eye,
One of the things you could never do about it is lie.

Amber Kennedy (11)
St Leonard's CE Primary School, Preston

Hatred

Hatred is as red as blood
It sounds like a machine gun purring
Hatred spits out insults
It lashes out at everything
Hatred wants revenge
Hatred loathes love
Its friend is anger
It spreads bad rumours
Hatred's rage is like fire
It is like a poison
Hatred is cruel and uncaring
It radiates a nasty, loathsome aura
Plants die around Hatred
Stealing gifts that are given to others
As bitter as lemon
Nobody but Anger likes Hatred
Hatred lurks in dark places
Has Hatred got you?

Matthew Barker (11)
St Leonard's CE Primary School, Preston

My Happy Life

I'm always happy, I'm never sad,
I'm always good, I'm never bad.
I love playing outside, up and down my slide,
I also play with my hula-hoop, it's like a giant ring.
I spin it round and round my middle,
But it just falls down and makes me giggle.
I love playing basketball but always miss the net,
I throw it high I throw it low,
It always ends up on my toe.
I also love to sing and dance,
And do handstands on my head.
At the end of the day I'm very tired,
And just want to flop in bed.

Chloe Cowley (10)
St Leonard's CE Primary School, Preston

Opposite Emotions

H olidays out in the shining sun

A lways having lots of fun

P laying games with my fabulous friends

P arty time never ends

Y es, this makes me happy

S eeing people leaving me out

A nyone who likes to shout

D oing homework when I would rather play out

N ot getting my own way with my sister, Holly

E very time I see sad things on TV

S aying goodbye to my fantastic family

S o all of these things make me sad.

Amy Trumper (9)
St Leonard's CE Primary School, Preston

Happiness Is Football

I love playing football,
I feel like I can score a hat-trick every day.
I feel happy when my best friend, Tom, scores,
It is like a dream come true when we win tournaments,
I hear our parents cheering loudly.

I love going to watch matches, it makes me feel happy,
The crowd go wild when we score,
My favourite football team is Preston,
I felt so happy when Preston beat Sheffield,
I jumped up and down,
When the whistle goes and my team have won,
I feel horrendously happy.

Matthew Clark (7)
St Leonard's CE Primary School, Preston

Love

You look for me then think I'm not there,
It's as if you're blind because I'm everywhere.

If only my sweet scent of sweet roses was recognised
When the innocent boy hugged his golden dog
Below the vibrant, angelic butterflies.

If only you heard my soft bells ring,
When the elderly woman watered her emerald tree
And began to sing.

If only you knew when we were to meet,
When the parents of yours were to meet you
A baby so sweet.

Ailah Hamid (11)
St Leonard's CE Primary School, Preston

Happy Days!

H appiness is playing in the warm sun,

A ltogether, building sandcastles is such fun,

P icnics by the sea, watching boats passing by,

P atterned, brightly coloured kites waving through the sky,

Y ummy, scrummy ice creams dripping down my face,

D own by the rock pools is a really cool place,

A nemones, crabs, sea snails, tiny fish and seaweed,

Y ou can dive, swim, bodyboard and jump the waves,

S leepy but happy, it's the end of the day.

Joel Bird (8)
St Leonard's CE Primary School, Preston

I Feel Happy!

I feel happy,
Going to school,
Listening to the teachers.
Took part in PE today,
Where's the swimming pool?

I feel happy,
Playing on my computer,
Minecraft, FIFA, Call of Duty,
Spending lots of hours in a virtual world,
Build a city, score a goal,
Come on, you beauty!

I feel happy,
Playing with my friends,
Seeing their latest trends,
But wait a minute, viewing their fad,
I could have looked on my iPad.

Matthew Owen Mackie (10)
St Leonard's CE Primary School, Preston

An Exciting Christmas

I wonder what there will be under the Christmas tree.
I am in bed and excitement is starting to spread.
I can't wait for the tree,
I wonder what there will be.
Remember what it is all about,
Not the dinner, not presents - Jesus
And God is what it's all about.
Finally, it's the day, the day where we can play
and pray.
We have opened our presents with much noise
and chatter,
The school holidays are nearly over,
I can't wait to see my friends.

Amy Shamsuddin (10)
St Leonard's CE Primary School, Preston

My Birthday

It's my birthday soon as the flowers are starting
to bloom,
I can't wait to see all the presents that are waiting
for me.
I'm really excited,
My friends are coming home for tea and they are going
to spend time with me.
I'm happy and joyful as you can see.
I can't wait for my birthday tea.
I'm in bed and the excitement is starting to spread.
It's nearly the day I've been waiting for,
Although I have to share because I have a twin sister.

Hannah Shamsuddin (10)
St Leonard's CE Primary School, Preston

Anger Just Won't Hide

Deep underground
Lives an emotion
Called Anger.
He is fierce
He's ferocious
He scares people away.
Whoever gets the closest
Becomes more ferocious.

He arrived at school
One sunny, beaming day.
'Oh my!' he yells
And scares the birds away.
Children run and cry with fear
'Shush!' he yells
So they stand and wait for him to go underground
So he did and sat with a frown.

Erin McEwan (9)
St Leonard's CE Primary School, Preston

Anger!

If anger were a colour it would be red,
Like a pit of fire.

It would taste like a red-hot chilli
Burning in your mouth.

It would look spiky with a mad face,
Like the face of an angry teacher.

It would sound like thunder and lightning
Everywhere.

It would smell like smoke,
Getting worse and worse.

It would feel horrible and mean,
Like a storm gaining on you.

Holly Smith (11)
St Leonard's CE Primary School, Preston

Happy, Happy, Happiness

H is for happiness, happiness is ruby-red

A is for amazing times ahead

P is for pretty poppies, the sweet smell of happiness

P is for people playing

I is for ice lollies, the delicious taste of happiness

N is for noise, the sound of laughter, giggles and squeals. This is happiness to me!

E is for excitement, the lovely feeling inside

S is for sugar and spice, all things nice

S is for super, this is happiness to me.

Ruby-May Graves (9)
St Leonard's CE Primary School, Preston

What Emotion Am I?

I'm the whimpering dog in the back of your throat,
I'm the shivering zap going down your spine,
I'm the thoughts teleporting through your mind,
I'm in a rush when darkness comes.
I'm like Scooby-Doo and Shaggy when they're
running away
When I'm OK.
Now here, here is a mighty task,
If I may ask,
What emotion am I?

Now that I am calm,
My anger is under control,
My name is Anger.

Bradley Bowden
St Leonard's CE Primary School, Preston

Frustrated Freddie...

F reddie was frustrated at losing the game

R eferees are sometimes quick to blame

U sually my dad stands by my goal cheering me on

S aturday was the day we lost two-one

T uesday is the day we train, why oh why does it

R ain, rain, rain?

A pril was the month of our first game

T hat was our shot at football fame

E veryone on the team did their very best

D uring the game we all needed a rest.

Freddie Masterson (7)
St Leonard's CE Primary School, Preston

Joy In My Heart

When I bump into a surprise,
I can hardly believe my eyes.
Wherever it is,
I feel joy fill my heart.

Whether I write, draw or read,
I feel joy in my heart.
The challenge is the thing I like,
It makes it exciting.

Lucy Ashton (8)
St Leonard's CE Primary School, Preston

Untitled

Football gives me the most happiness,
Playing with my friends who are fabulous.
I always aim to get a hat-trick,
Playing so hard I am almost sick.
The best feeling is to score
And last week I banged in four.
Being a part of Bamber Bridge football team,
Lets me live the dream.
Dodging all the challengers,
Showing skills taught by managers.
Wanting to be as good as Dixie Dean,
One of the best players ever seen.

William Lane (8)
St Leonard's CE Primary School, Preston

Anger

No one likes him
He is always in the way
When he's around no one's there.

He won't go away
He is always mean and never keen
No one knows why he is here.

Everyone runs when he comes
He's as hot as the sun
He likes being mean but not very keen.

Why does anger have to be around?
I hate you more than baked beans!
Anger disappear, disappear!

Daniel Smith (9)
St Leonard's CE Primary School, Preston

The Happy Way Is The Only Way

If you smile it makes people happy,
Change their attitude when they're snappy,
The atmosphere changes when people are sad,
Make a difference, cheer them up today,
You could tell them some good old jokes.
If you are sad, ask advice from your folks,
Tell them, just remember you are lucky,
Some people are eating off their hands which
are mucky,
So put a smile upon your face,
For you're in a happy place.

Louis Wall (9)
St Leonard's CE Primary School, Preston

Anger

Anger makes you rage,
Anger makes you shout,
Anger makes you go to your room,
And we say that's unfair.

Anger lives deep, deep down,
All the way down your body,
It happens when you're in a fight,
Or even when you cry.

So now you know what anger is,
And also when you use it,
So instead of being mean and nasty,
Be kind and loyal to family and friends.

Evelina Kazlauskaite-Lee (9)
St Leonard's CE Primary School, Preston

My Frustration

I am often frustrated
Wishing I could have celebrated
A glorious hoop scoring three

I try to create
Even emulate
The other players on court

I frustrate
It's like I'm at a gate
And I don't want to be late
But when I get there, I simply hesitate

I want to create
I want to be great
Sinking a shot and scoring three!

Findley Dunne (8)
St Leonard's CE Primary School, Preston

Love

Love is when your family is here,
Love is when you shed a tear,
Love is when it is just me and Mum,
Love is when my dad can come,
Love is when Christmas is here,
Love is when Santa is near,
Love is seeing my gorgeous gran,
Love is dancing for my gran,
Love is like a big warm bath,
Love can always make you laugh,
Love is a perfect sound,
Love makes the world go round.

Lucy-Jane Bickerstaff (10)
St Leonard's CE Primary School, Preston

Anger

Raging like a furious bull,
Or kicking and screaming
At the top of my voice,
Hitting you and exploding.
The red cloud appears,
I stare happiness straight in the eye,
I am the cloud who rains and thunders,
Or even the spice of the hottest chilli.
I am the one who steals your sweets
And trips you up and laughs near your feet,
The monster of destruction I am.
For I am Anger!

Joshua McGee (11)
St Leonard's CE Primary School, Preston

Fear

Fear threatens you to scream and run
It sticks in your mind for the rest of your life
It creeps around in the pitch dark of night
It hides in the corner until the time is right
It reminds you of times when you were afraid
and alone
It taps on your window and makes you shiver
and shake
It finds you no matter where you hide
For this is Fear
And it lives in everyone.

Megan Tinniswood (11)
St Leonard's CE Primary School, Preston

Frustrations In My Life

I feel very frustrated when my homework is due in.
My mum, she makes me do it!
I really cannot win.

When I'm in the goal,
As goalkeeping is my role,
I feel very frustrated when the striker scores a goal.

At bedtime I feel frustrated,
When Dad says, 'Bedtime, Leo!'
I'd rather watch TV and not have my head down on
my pillow.

Leo Lewis (10)
St Leonard's CE Primary School, Preston

Rainbow Emotions

Red is for anger I feel when my football team loses.
Yellow is for cheerfulness in the air.
Pink is for loving children playing in the street.
Green is for adventurous people who explore the wild.
Orange makes me feel hungry for tasty fruit.
Purple is for magical dragons and wizards.
Blue gives me energetic powers like Superman.
I feel different emotions from the colours of a rainbow.

Lewis Hammonds (7)
St Leonard's CE Primary School, Preston

If Happy Were...

If happy were a colour, it would be yellow,
As bright as the sun on a spring morning,
If happy were a taste, it would be just like rich
dark chocolate
Melting on your tongue.
If happy were a feeling, it would be playing in the deep
blue sea.
If happy were a smell, it would be freshly
baked muffins.
If happy were a sound, it would be the birds tweeting in
the trees.

Oliver Healy (10)
St Leonard's CE Primary School, Preston

Happy Holiday

Holidays make me happy
Visiting vicious volcanoes
Smelling salty seas
Licking lush lollies
Diving down deep
Slip, slap, slopping suncream
Flip-flop feet
Fast, squidgy squid
Lots of laughing lads
Giggling girls
Swinging swings
Tall trampolines
Fluttering flags
Special sandcastles
Holidays make me happy.

Joshua Cockburn (8)
St Leonard's CE Primary School, Preston

Excusive Embarrassment

The dog ate my homework,
The newsletter's in the bin,
The car got stuck in traffic,
'That litter's not mine!'

The fairies messed up my bedroom,
And opened the cupboard doors,
Don't pick flowers or they won't survive,
Stop embarrassing me!

I don't own that dirty car,
Just leave me alone.

Hannah Elizabeth Tuton (8)
St Leonard's CE Primary School, Preston

Happy Times

Free as a bee,
I dance in the sun,
I'd dance in the rain,
In the snow and the hail.

Snug as a mouse,
I read on my chair,
I get lost in the book,
Through imagining worlds my mind travels.

These things make me happy,
Whatever the mood,
I'd be lost without them,
In my own complete world.

Alice Wilton (8)
St Leonard's CE Primary School, Preston

Your Emotions

Hope:
Keep on hoping because luck might come your way,
Whatever you are hoping for might appear the very
next day.

Fear:
Don't be scared of your fear because it can make
us strong,
Embrace it, overcome it, put it in a song.

So here is a little poem to help you on your way,
Life is full of emotions each and every day.

Amy Jessica Butler
St Leonard's CE Primary School, Preston

The Day We Won The Cup

Weak, but then strong,
Sad, but then happy,
We were feeling hopeful,
The crowd were all clapping.

Scared and uncertain,
When will it end?
They were running at us,
We had to defend.

The ref blew the whistle,
The twenty minutes were up,
We all stood on the podium,
To lift the Legia Cup.

Thomas Keith Myles (10)
St Leonard's CE Primary School, Preston

Fear

I turn you into a shocking mess of fears,
I'm a deep purple emotion giving you tension,
Not to mention when I haunted your sleep,
I kept coming back so you don't count sheep,
I am under your bed waiting for you to sleep,
So I can enter your head giving you frightening scares,
I give you nightmares,
Take away your cares,
I am Fear.

Ellie Louise Barton (11)
St Leonard's CE Primary School, Preston

How I Am Always Angry

My anger acts like some blazing magma,
I hate everyone and everything.
I am known for taking people's anger from inside.
I am never happy, scared, disgusted or sad.
Steam bursts out of my earholes,
Everyone is afraid of me.
I never go to school,
I never listen to anyone.
I will not do any work.

I am Anger!

Kai Jones
St Leonard's CE Primary School, Preston

The Children's Life Which Is All They Do Is Play Outside

The children play while the sun shines,
The children play while the church bells chime,
The children play on a very special day,
The children play in May,
The children play at making their own games,
The children play and make their own names,
The children play while their dads are lazy,
The children play with their best friend, Maisy.

Imogen Crankshaw (9)
St Leonard's CE Primary School, Preston

If You're Feeling Worried

If you're feeling worried, no need to be scared
Go to a teacher and they will be there.

If you're feeling worried, no need to feel down
If you're feeling worried, no need to frown.

If you're feeling worried, no need to cry
Go to your friend, you will be fine.
If you're feeling worried.

Phoebe Tinniswood (8)
St Leonard's CE Primary School, Preston

It's My Birthday!

I'm so excited, it's my birthday,
I want to shout, 'Hooray, hooray!'
I can't wait for my party to get on its way!
I want everyone to stay and play.

I'm so excited, it's my birthday,
It's going to be my day,
With lots of presents on the way,
I want it to last for a year and a day.

Abigail Parker (8)
St Leonard's CE Primary School, Preston

Happiness

H atfulls of laughter

A nd tummies full of giggles

P laying with my friends

P lenty of fun to enjoy

I n the games we play

N o time for sadness

E nd the day with glee

S oon it will be time for us to come in for our tea

S leeping now, enjoying a nice dream.

Zak Billington (7)
St Leonard's CE Primary School, Preston

Jumping Joy

I like to smile and dance about,
When I do the right thing, I feel proud.
My body feels as light as a butterfly,
When I see my friends and we are playing around.

I like to laugh and have lots of fun,
Have you ever been sad or left alone?
What makes you feel 'wow' instead.
What emotion am I?

Amy Knight Garcia (9)
St Leonard's CE Primary School, Preston

Splashy, Splashy Sea

I'm in the splashy-splashy sea,
The sea went in my mouth.
I like salt on my chips
But not on my tongue!

Waaaa!
The wet blanket went in my eyes,
I'm blind!

No, no, no!
The sea found my perfect sandcastle.
Waaa!
The seagull ate my ice lolly!

Harry Joe Noonan (9)
St Leonard's CE Primary School, Preston

What I Did This Morning

I woke up today with nothing to do,
I felt sad as any of us would do,
I went for my breakfast, that cheered me up,
I soon was a butterfly, good as gold,
I got into my clothes, my mood going down,
But soon almost everything changed around,
I was now happy, very, very good,
Wow! What a fantastic morning it was!

Hannah Sergeant (10)
St Leonard's CE Primary School, Preston

Happiness

Happiness is yellow, like the sun shining on the beach,
Happiness smells nice and fresh,
Happiness tastes like candyfloss that you buy from theme parks,
Happiness looks like a bright yellow bouncy ball glued in the sky,
Happiness sounds like birds tweeting on a warm summer's day,
Happiness feels like winning the lottery!

Rebecca Freeman (11)
St Leonard's CE Primary School, Preston

You Can Be Happy When You're...

You can be happy when you're eating an ice cream,
You can be happy when you're having a nice dream,
You can be happy when you're having a sing-song,
You can be happy when you're playing a little game
of ping-pong,
You can be happy when you're having a good day,
You can be happy any time, hey!

Josh Southern (10)
St Leonard's CE Primary School, Preston

Fishing

I love fishing, there is no doubt,
Nothing makes me happier than catching a shiny
rainbow trout.
With rod in hand and landing net ready, bring it in nice
and steady,
That's what makes me happy.
At first it's calm and going slow, suddenly starts to pull
the adrenalin,
Starts with my heart beating faster.

George Yerkess (10)
St Leonard's CE Primary School, Preston

Excited Is Good!

E xcited is the best emotion you can ever feel.

M any times I feel it at an evening meal.

O ccasionally it makes me tingle.

T aste the flavours beginning to mingle.

I move my feet to the beat.

O ften before I have meat!

N ow excited is the best emotion ever.

Jessica Hurst
St Leonard's CE Primary School, Preston

Angry Anger

A ll the people be happy

N ever be angry when you get told off because you
will never get away with it

G o and be calm and never get angry because you get
to do fun things when you're calm

E xcited, energetic and always happy

R emember, never get angry and always be happy.

George Holt (9)
St Leonard's CE Primary School, Preston

I'm Feeling Stressed

I could slam my door
I could rip my paper up
I cannot stand this

I could stomp away
I could throw things on the floor
I cannot calm down

I can't stop smiling
It's like my mouth's fixed together
It's a happy time.

Varissa Surti (9)
St Leonard's CE Primary School, Preston

Anger

Anger is like red puffs of smoke coming out of
your ears.
It tastes like red-hot chillies.
It smells like the smoke of a burning barn.
It looks like a nuclear bomb, ready to blow up.
It sounds like sparks from a bonfire.
It feels like the world is going to set on fire.

Oliver McGee
St Leonard's CE Primary School, Preston

Fear

Fear is an empty room.
Fear is a dark street.
Fear is a lonely island.
Fear is a deserted desert.
Fear is a haunted house.
Fear is a pair of razor-sharp teeth.
Fear is a scary monster.
Fear is a dark corridor.
Fear is a dark, empty field.

Jensen D C Hull (11)
St Leonard's CE Primary School, Preston

Anger

A nger is a feeling that no one likes to have,

N othing makes me angrier than people getting on my nerves,

G ames, like Frustration, really anger people,

E ndermen in Minecraft get mad if you stare,

R omans got angry under the emperor's rule.

William Thomas Steven (10)
St Leonard's CE Primary School, Preston

Who Is Happiness?

Happiness is good, happiness is great,
It makes you laugh, it makes you smile,
It even makes you cry tears of joy.
I like joking, frog-like croaking.
My brother likes maths,
My mum likes baths,
All these things make people happy,
Especially me!

Grace Connolly
St Leonard's CE Primary School, Preston

Footballers

I am a footballer before a football match,
I am a footballer that is in a cup final,
I am a footballer losing an important match,
I am a footballer whose team is on the edge of
relegation,
I am a footballer who is having to retire.

Tense...

Jack John Massey (11)
St Leonard's CE Primary School, Preston

Inside Out

What's on your mind?
If I turned you inside out,
What would I see?
What's up?
I need to know!

What's on your mind?
I really don't know.
We need to bind.
What's up?
I need to know!

Jorja Simpson (9)
St Leonard's CE Primary School, Preston

He's Happy

H appy to me is spending time with my family,

A t the restaurant spending time with my family,

P lay with family while watching the dogs run,

P laying with family is like having one million pounds,

Y ou always like to chat with family.

Benjamin Harmel (10)
St Leonard's CE Primary School, Preston

Happy Happiness

I am happy in the summer,
I am happy in the spring,
I am happy on the playground,
I am happy on the swing.

I am happy on my scooter,
I am happy on my bike,
I am happy in the sun,
I am happy having fun.

Katie Hanna (9)
St Leonard's CE Primary School, Preston

Sadness

Sadness tastes like the salty sea.

Sadness looks like a gloomy forest.

It sounds like thousands of birds screeching.

It smells like a bowl of salt.

It is a dark blue colour.

It feels like tiny men inside you, punching your chest.

Joseph Benson (11)
St Leonard's CE Primary School, Preston

When I'm Alone

Standing on the playground
With nobody around
I stand, I watch, I listen to the sound
Of children playing happily
And running around
Like a horse race going by
But then there's only me
Nobody will play.

Emilia Alice Fox (7)
St Leonard's CE Primary School, Preston

Happiness

Happiness tastes sweet like vanilla ice cream.
It smells sweet like roses.
Its colour is light blue like the sky.
You feel it when the sun is shining and it is warm.
You feel it when you wake up on the first day of
a holiday.

Kathryn Lord (11)
St Leonard's CE Primary School, Preston

Happiness Comes To Me

Happiness comes to me,
Even when I don't look or see.

When I play with my friends,
Happiness comes to me.

Happiness comes to me the most,
When I'm with my mum and my dad.

Tom Ashton (7)
St Leonard's CE Primary School, Preston

My Garden

H ow I love my garden

A nd its weeping willow

P ractising tennis with my dad

P inging the tennis ball against the wall

Y ummy treats my mum will bring, I could not want another thing.

James Edward Steven (8)
St Leonard's CE Primary School, Preston

Fear Surrounds You

Fear surrounds you,
It's everywhere you go,
Ferocious fear,
Just go, go, go!
You're filled with happiness
Or you're filled with fear,
So run, run, run
From Mr Fear!

Olivia Chatterton (9)
St Leonard's CE Primary School, Preston

Happiness

Happiness is pink, like fluffy marshmallows.
It tastes like sweet sugar.
It smells nice and sticky.
It looks like pink cats running around.
It sounds like birds tweeting.
Happiness is wonderful.

Reece Crossley (10)
St Leonard's CE Primary School, Preston

Fear Is Black

Fear is black, like the night.
It tastes like rotten meat.
It smells old and soggy.
It looks like your worst nightmare.
It sounds like a cat scraping a plate.
Fear feels like it will never end.

Eleanor Jane Boardman (11)
St Leonard's CE Primary School, Preston

Happiness

Happiness is spending time with your family.
It feels like you're on a winning team.
It tastes sweet and yummy.
It smells like fresh air.
Love is happiness
And I have happiness inside me.

Sam Craven (10)
St Leonard's CE Primary School, Preston

Happiness

I make people happy when they are sad
I immediately take away the anger and swap it with joy.
I never take or steal, I always let you keep
Even when you can't see me I am with you.
I am happiness.

James Robert Smith (10)
St Leonard's CE Primary School, Preston

Happy Times!

Ice cream in the park
On a hot summer's day
The joy of friends
We laugh and play

And if it rains
We run inside
And paint a picture
Of happier times!

Ruby Guttridge (9)
St Leonard's CE Primary School, Preston

Peace

P eople should be allowed peace.

E nd bad things that happen to us.

A llowed to have our own minds.

C onfidence in other people.

E veryone in the world should be happy.

Jacob Regan (8)
St Leonard's CE Primary School, Preston

Fear

I am waiting for you under your bed.
I am the feeling in your stomach when you're in the sky.
I am why you don't want to go on stage.
I am the reason you don't like spiders.
I am Fear.

Charlie Smith (11)
St Leonard's CE Primary School, Preston

Anger

I boil your blood, making your face turn bright red.
I throw my pencil at the teacher when I am mad.
I tear books when I don't like them.
I am irritating.
I am a devil.
I am Anger.

Joshua Clifford (10)
St Leonard's CE Primary School, Preston

Happy Emotions

Happy emotions can help you do lots of fun things.
They help you do things funnily and emotionally.
They make you active and smile.
Happy emotions are things that can make
you entertaining.

Noah Patchell (10)
St Leonard's CE Primary School, Preston

Anger

My brother winds me up,
My heart pounds,
Feet stamp,
Smash, crash,
The door slams,
Crying in bed,
Shouting into my pillow,
Feeling guilty,
Creep downstairs,
Say sorry,
Everything better...
Until next time.

Jensen Garnett (8)
St Paul's CE Junior School, Barrow-In-Furness

Love

We're on our way to Blackpool
To go and fetch our dog.
On the way we got her a toy hog.
I gave it to her, she chewed it well.
Oh my gosh,
This dog is swell!
I love her
She is so cool,
I'm sure this dog is going to rule!

Alessia Rigg (8)
St Paul's CE Junior School, Barrow-In-Furness

Star Of The Week

I'm sitting and listening,
I wonder who it's going to be?
'... and the star of the week is Jay!'
'Yay, it's me!'
She gives me a certificate and I feel proud.

Jay White (8)
St Paul's CE Junior School, Barrow-In-Furness

About Me

I am a joyful boy,
Sometimes I am crazy.
I am the crazy kid at home.
I am a nice boy.
Sometimes I am silly.
I am best friends with,
Josh, Oliver, Jamie and Alessia.

Oliver Ducie (7)
St Paul's CE Junior School, Barrow-In-Furness

Sad

Crying, my cousin winds me up
I cover myself up
My mum hugs me
She cheers me up!
We play Monopoly
Four in a row
Doctor, Doctor
It is fun.

Daniel Johnson (8)
St Paul's CE Junior School, Barrow-In-Furness

Happy

When I'm happy I'm jumping with joy
When I'm happy I'm excited as can be
When I'm happy you can tell
Because I'm all of these things.

Oliver Goodwin (7)
St Paul's CE Junior School, Barrow-In-Furness

Untitled

When I'm happy, the sun comes out,
When I'm happy, I love to play,
When I'm joyful, I run around,
When I'm happy, I love the day!

Cameron Duke (7)
St Paul's CE Junior School, Barrow-In-Furness

Grumpy

Sister shouting,
Chores to do,
Now I'm just nagging you.
Screaming, shouting, slamming the door,
This is what I need to ignore.

Violet Bland (8)
St Paul's CE Junior School, Barrow-In-Furness

Panic

My heart pounds,
I run home,
I tear the door open,
I look around...
No one there...
Or is there?

Jamie Jackson (8)
St Paul's CE Junior School, Barrow-In-Furness

Fear

I am loved in my heart,
I have fear of the dark,
People panic,
But I don't,
Inside me I feel loved.

Lily Rose Milburn (7)
St Paul's CE Junior School, Barrow-In-Furness

Emotions Poem

My brothers, they're horrible to me,
Kick me,
Push me,
They say horrible things to me,
I feel sad.

Jordan Neale (7)
St Paul's CE Junior School, Barrow-In-Furness

Untitled

I went to a shop
Called 'Game'
It wasn't fun
I did not like it
Bored and disappointed!

Reece Metcalfe (7)
St Paul's CE Junior School, Barrow-In-Furness

Est.1991

Young Writers Information

We hope you have enjoyed reading this book – and that you will continue to in the coming years.

If you're a young writer who enjoys reading and creative writing, or the parent of an enthusiastic poet or story writer, do visit our website www.youngwriters.co.uk. Here you will find free competitions, workshops and games, as well as recommended reads, a poetry glossary and our blog.

If you would like to order further copies of this book, or any of our other titles, then please give us a call or visit **www.youngwriters.co.uk.**

Young Writers
Remus House
Coltsfoot Drive
Peterborough
PE2 9BF
(01733) 890066 / 898110
info@youngwriters.co.uk